Panther Medium Tank 1942–45

Stephen A Hart • Illustrated by Jim Laurier

First published in Great Britain in 2003 by Osprey Publishing,
Elms Court, Chapel Way, Botley, Oxford OX2 9LP, United Kingdom.
Email: info@ospreypublishing.com

ISBN 1 84176 543 0

Editor: Simone Drinkwater
Design: Melissa Orrom Swan
Index by Alison Worthington
Originated by Grasmere Digital Imaging, Leeds, UK
Printed in China through World Print Ltd.

03 04 05 06 07   10 9 8 7 6 5 4 3 2 1

For a catalogue of all books published by Osprey Military and Aviation please
contact:

Osprey Direct UK, P.O. Box 140, Wellingborough, Northants, NN8 2FA, UK
E-mail: info@ospreydirect.co.uk

Osprey Direct USA, c/o MBI Publishing, P.O. Box 1, 729 Prospect Ave,
Osceola, WI 54020, USA
E-mail: info@ospreydirectusa.com

www.ospreypublishing.com

Artist's note

Readers may care to note that the original paintings from which the colour
plates in this book were prepared are available for private sale. All reproduction
copyright whatsoever is retained by the Publishers. All enquiries should be
addressed to:

Jim Laurier, 85 Carroll Street, Keene, New Hampshire, NH 03431, USA

The Publishers regret that they can enter into no correspondence upon this
matter.

PANTHER MEDIUM TANK 1942–45

DEVELOPMENT HISTORY

The origins of the Panther tank lay in the shock that the German Army experienced during Operation Barbarossa – its June 1941 invasion of the Soviet Union. During the first week of combat, the otherwise triumphant German Panzer spearheads experienced fierce encounters with the Soviet T-34/76 medium tank. Although the T-34/76 was in short supply at the front in 1941, it nevertheless outclassed every German tank then in service. With its combination of excellent mobility, mechanical reliability, potent firepower, and effective, well-sloped armour protection, the T-34 posed a formidable threat to the success of Barbarossa. Several tactical engagements during the campaign demonstrated the superiority of the T-34, particularly the severe blow experienced by the 4th Panzer Division at Mtsensk, near Orel, on 4 October 1941.

This division belonged to Colonel-General Heinz Guderian's Panzer Group 2, which spearheaded the German Army Group Centre. In the aftermath of the setback at Mtsensk, Guderian demanded that an inquiry

The shock the Germans experienced after encountering the Soviet T-34/76 tank during Operation Barbarossa led them to develop the Panther, which incorporated the overhanging gun barrel, well-sloped armoured plates, and large road wheels featured in the enemy tank. (The Tank Museum, 47/E6)

be established into the realities of tank warfare on the Eastern Front. During 18–21 November, senior German tank designers and manufacturers, plus staff officers from the Army Weapons Department, toured Guderian's operational area to study captured T-34 tanks and to evaluate the implications that this vehicle posed for future German tank development. Guderian suggested to the inquiry that Germany should simply produce a

direct copy of the T-34 tank, as this would be the quickest way of countering the threat that this vehicle posed. The Weapons Department disagreed, however, because Germany would find it difficult to produce steel alloy and diesel engines in sufficient quantities. While deliberations on a new tank unfolded, the inquiry recommended that the Army up-gunned its Panzer IV tanks and Sturmgeschütz III assault guns.

The answer, however, as the inquiry recognised, was to incorporate the best features of the T-34 into a new German medium tank. The inquiry – now known as the Panther Commission – concluded that the T-34's main strengths revolved around three features that to date had been lacking in German tank design. The Soviet tank's main armament overhung the front of the vehicle, which enabled it to have a greater barrel length and thus deliver a higher muzzle velocity to its rounds; consequently, the weapon obtained increased armour penetration capabilities. Second, the suspension on the T-34 featured large road wheels and wide tracks that gave the vehicle excellent off-road mobility and an impressive maximum road speed. Last, while the Soviet tank had only modestly thick armour (with 45mm plates), these were well sloped and so gave greater levels of protection than German tanks with vertical armoured plates of similar thickness.

In late November 1941, the Panther Commission contracted the armaments firms of Daimler-Benz and Maschinenfabrik Augsberg-Nuremburg (MAN) to begin development work on a new tank in the 30-tonne class, designated the VK30.02. Each firm's pro-

ABOVE **The 150th Panzer Brigade employed 10 Panthers disguised as American M10 tank destroyers to spread confusion during the initial stages of the mid-December 1944 German Ardennes counter-offensive. (The Tank Museum, 1164/A2)**

BELOW **This mid-production Model A Panther has been overturned, presumably by Allied aerial bombing, at Norrey-en-Bessin during the summer 1944 Normandy campaign. Note the twin cooling pipes added to the vehicle's left exhaust pipe. (The Tank Museum, 5721/F6)**

totypes were to mount the turret then being developed by Rheinmetall that featured the long-barrelled 7.5cm L/70 gun. On 9 December 1941, the Weapons Department set the specified weight of the VK30.02 at 32.5 tonnes. During spring 1942, Daimler-Benz completed three slightly different versions of their prototype design, the VK30.02(DB). These vehicles had a sloping hull design, forward-mounted turret, overhanging main gun, and large square gun mantlet that all bore a strong resemblance to the T-34. In addition, one of these three prototypes had a diesel engine similar to that fitted in the Soviet tank, although here driven through a rear sprocket. However, unlike the T-34, the VK30.02(DB) featured the traditional German suspension design based on bogie wheels mounted on external leaf springs that had been used on the previous Panzer I–IV tanks. The VK30.02(DB) weighed 35 tonnes, had sloped armour up to 60mm thick, and delivered an operational by-road range of 195km. The vehicle's relatively narrow tracks, however, produced an unimpressively high ground pressure figure of $0.83kg/cm^2$.

In comparison, the VK30.02(MAN) design represented less of a direct copy of the T-34 and had much in common with earlier German tanks. In terms of the vehicle's overall shape, only its sloped glacis front plate represented design copied from the T-34. The three MAN prototype vehicles in turn used an MB502 diesel engine, or one of two traditional German petrol engines – the 650bhp Maybach HL210 and 700bhp HL230 – all with an orthodox drive train that ran under the fighting compartment to the gearbox. The suspensions on the MAN prototypes, however, owed little to typical German tank design. The vehicles had eight large road wheel bogies that used a sophisticated internal twin torsion bar system instead of the more usual German external leaf spring system. By locating the turret in the centre of the tank, the VK30.02(MAN) design minimised the degree to which the gun barrel overhung the front of the tank. The MAN prototypes weighed the same as the Daimler-Benz vehicles, yet their larger (750 litre) fuel tanks delivered a greater by-road operating range of 270km and their wider tracks a more favourable ground pressure figure of $0.68kg/cm^2$.

After evaluating the designs, Hitler concluded that the Daimler-Benz prototypes were superior, but on 11 May the Weapons Department recommended acceptance of the MAN proposal. This was because the

Department feared that friendly-fire incidents would arise because the VK30.02(DB) looked too similar to the T-34, and that the long overhang of the main armament might result in vehicles getting their gun jammed into the ground when moving down slopes. Moreover, as the Daimler-Benz chassis possessed a narrower turret ring than the MAN version, this complicated the fitting of the Rheinmetall turret with its 7.5cm gun onto the vehicle.

Consequently, on 15 May 1942, the Army contracted MAN to produce the first pre-production versions of the new tank, now designated the Panzerkampfwagen V Panther Ausführung (or Model) A (Sdkfz 171), the tank's name deriving from the Panther Commission that had initiated the project back in late 1941. In January 1943, however, the Germans redesignated this first general production vehicle as the Panther Model D. The contracts issued in May included several modifications to the vehicle's specifications, most notably a front glacis plate with armour thickened from 60mm to 80mm. But concerns lingered within the High Command that the new Panther tank would be inadequately protected against the weapons likely to appear on the Eastern Front in the foreseeable future. Therefore, on 4 June 1942, Hitler suggested that the frontal armour of the Model D be increased to 100mm. Experiments revealed, however, that adding additional bolt-on armoured plates to the existing Panther design (as done previously on the Panzer III and IV) would pose enormous technical difficulties. This in turn led the Germans to halt these up-armouring proposals and instead consider the development of a redesigned and up-armoured Panther tank, subsequently designated the Panther II.

During August 1942, MAN produced two prototype Panthers for evaluation, designated Versuchs (Experimental) Panther Vehicles V1 and V2. The V1 was just a chassis without a turret fitted, whereas the V2 was a complete tank. The latter featured an unusual hexagonal turret that mounted the Rheinmetall 7.5cm KwK 42 L/70 gun with a single-baffle muzzle brake – whereas all subsequent Panther tanks featured a double-baffle brake. In addition, the rear left of the vehicle's turret had a distinctive drum-shaped commander's cupola that visibly bulged out beyond the face of the turret's left-hand side plates.

During 8–14 November, the Germans tested the V2 tank at proving grounds near Eisenach in Germany. While these tests showed the design to be sound in general, they nevertheless exposed the many technical problems from which the V2 suffered. Over-hasty design and production work, for example, meant that the V2 vehicle weighed 43 tonnes, well above the target weight limit of 35 tonnes. One reason for this excessive weight was that during the development stage Hitler had insisted that the vehicle's frontal armour be increased from the stipulated 60mm thickness to 80mm. With its 650bhp Maybach engine, the V2 tank delivered a power-to-weight ratio of just 15.1bhp/tonne – 15 per cent lower than the figure for the T-34 tank and 25 per cent lower than that of the original VK30.02(MAN). This excessive weight-to-power ratio caused numerous mechanical problems – especially excessive strain on the wheels, engine, gearbox and transmission – that dogged the Model D Panther throughout its nine-month production run.

The subsequent modifications that the Germans implemented during the Panther Model D and Model A production runs alleviated these problems, and thus in the Model G Panther the Germans arrived at a mechanically more reliable tank. Nevertheless, they never entirely

This early Model D Panther sports two features that distinguish it from later Model D tanks – its smoke-grenade launchers and the two shrouded lamps located on the hull glacis plate. Two features characteristic of Model D or early Model A Panthers are also evident – the tall letterbox machine gun mount on the right glacis plate and the oblong driver's visor on the left glacis plate. (The Tank Museum, 22/C2)

solved these weaknesses prior to the war's end in May 1945, and this unreliability somewhat undermined the tank's obvious benefits – notably the combination of a potent 7.5cm gun and well-sloped armour. During late 1942, however, the Germans were desperate to get their new Panther tank into combat on the Eastern Front. Consequently, despite the many flaws exposed during the Eisenach trials, the Army rushed the V2 design straight into general production as the Model D Panther. With the benefit of hindsight, it is clear that the Germans ought to have ironed out these design problems through a series of modified pre-production vehicles before rushing prematurely into general production. As it was, although significant numbers of completed Model D Panthers reached the Army during spring 1943, it remained far from clear that these vehicles were ready for use in combat.

PANTHER MODEL D

During late November 1942, the Germans embarked on general production of the V2 design, now designated the Panther Model D. Indeed, as far back as July 1942, the High Command had set a target figure of 250 Panthers to be delivered by 12 May 1943. Consequently, between November 1942 and January 1943, MAN produced the first four production Model D tanks. During 24–26 January 1943, three of these vehicles arrived at the Grafenwöhr testing grounds with the fourth going to Kummersdorf. The Model D production version featured a redesigned turret that lacked the hexagonal shape of the V2 turret, and which incorporated the commander's cupola positioned flush with the surface of the turret's left-hand side. In addition, the Model D mounted a modified 7.5cm KwK 42 L/70 gun that sported a double-baffle muzzle brake. In terms of secondary armament, the tank

The mid-production Model D Panther chassis number 213101, completed by MNH in late May or early June 1943, lacked smoke-grenade launchers but sported the more powerful 700bhp engine. This tank fought at Kursk where the Soviets captured it and then sent it to Britain, where this picture was taken. (The Tank Museum, 2389/D4)

This early Model D Panther fought in Operation Citadel during July 1943. Its tactical designation, painted in red with a white outline, identifies it as the fourth vehicle of the second platoon of the eighth company in one of the two Panther battalions employed in the offensive. (The Tank Museum, 22/B6)

mounted one 7.92mm MG 34 machine gun co-axially in the right of the turret mantlet, plus a hull machine gun that fired through a letterbox mount in the sloping hull glacis plate. The vehicle carried 79 rounds for the main gun and 4200 rounds for its machine guns. Finally, the tank mounted a set of three smoke-grenade launchers on the front of each turret side for close-range defence.

The Model D Panther had armour similar to the V2, except that the frontal glacis plate was 80mm thick and sloped at 55 degrees, while the hull side plates were 40mm thick and set at 40 degrees. The tank mounted the 650bhp Maybach HL210 P30 engine and the seven-speed AK 7-200 transmission used in the V2. Thanks to the additional armour protection, the Model D weighed 44.8 tonnes, slightly heavier than the already overweight V2 prototype. Nevertheless, the vehicle's torsion bar suspension, which was based on eight pairs of interleaved rubber-tyred road wheels, still delivered an acceptable ground pressure figure of 0.735kg/cm². The tank's by-road fuel consumption was 2.8 litres per kilometre which, given its 720 litre fuel tanks, enabled it to achieve a maximum operational range of 250km by road, yet just 100km off road. In terms of communications equipment, the Model D mounted the standard German tank device, the Fu 5. This consisted of a 10-watt transmitter with ultra-short wavelength receiver, operating in the frequency band 27.2–33.4MHz, that used a two-metre rod antenna fitted onto the vehicle's rear hull decking.

These first four Panthers underwent extensive tests at Grafenwöhr and Kummersdorf during late January and early February 1943, to be joined by further vehicles over the next few weeks. However, these tests – carried out by the crews of two new armoured units, the 51st and 52nd Panzer Battalions – revealed numerous minor design faults, as well as shoddy standards of manufacture. The gun, for example, could not be elevated or depressed to the specified degrees, while the corners of the turret often struck the closed driver's and radio operator's hatches on the hull roof. Furthermore, the vehicle's final drive chains tended to break, its transmission frequently broke down, its motors often caught fire and its fuel pumps regularly failed. The unseemly haste to rush the vehicle into general production had resulted, inevitably, in myriad teething problems.

During February 1943, despite these problems, MAN delivered a further 11 completed Panthers to the proving grounds, while Daimler-Benz completed its first six Panthers and MNH one further vehicle. By 28 February 1943, therefore, the Germans had delivered 22 Model D tanks to the two new Panther battalions. Thereafter, newly produced Panthers featured a fixed radius steering gear instead of the clutch-brake steering gear fitted in the first 22 Panthers. During March, Daimler-Benz, MAN, and MNH delivered 58 Model D Panthers to the Army, while Henschel completed its first ten tanks, so that by the end of the month the Germans had 90 such tanks on strength. But as yet the Germans had not passed a single Model D tank as combat-ready since the early trials had identified 45 modifications that needed to be made before the tank could be used in battle. At this time, the High Command believed that the Panther would make a decisive contribution to the strategic victory that the planned German summer 1943 offensive in the East was expected to achieve. During early April, however, the Army concluded that before this could happen it had to rebuild its completed Panthers to rectify the faults identified during the early field trials.

The Soviets captured this early Model D Panther of the 51st Panzer Battalion during the abortive July 1943 German Citadel offensive. Hitler expected that the 200 Panthers deployed for the attack would prove decisive, but in reality the Panther's combat debut was disappointing. (The Tank Museum, 143/C5)

The Germans, however, remained anxious that the modification work should not slow down the rate of completion of the part-assembled Panther tanks already on the production lines. Consequently, the four firms then producing Panthers did not take back the 90 vehicles already completed for modification work, but instead continued manufacturing Model D vehicles according to the original design despite its known faults. Only after 160 incomplete tanks had been finished would the Germans send them to the DEMAG factory at Falkensee for post-production modification work. In the interim, the 90 tanks already delivered would remain with the 51st and 52nd Panzer Battalions for training purposes and would only be dispatched to Falkensee for modification once the subsequent 160 completed Panthers had been rebuilt at DEMAG. The rebuilding work undertaken by the latter firm during April and May included major modifications to the engine compartment, adjustment to the steering gears, suspension, final drives and transmission. Although the German firms completed these remaining 160 Panthers essentially to the original design, they did at least make one modification to them. From April 1943 the factories outfitted new vehicles with thin Schürzen armoured side skirts to protect the relatively vulnerable tracks and hull sides from Soviet anti-tank rifles.

These five Panthers include one mid-production Model D vehicle (nearest the camera) that sports one shrouded head light, and four earlier Model D tanks each with two such lights. The factories deleted the second lamp from July 1943 as an economy measure. (The Tank Museum, 2902/D4)

By early May, frenzied German production had delivered the first batch of 250 Model D tanks to the proving grounds. In all subsequent construction, from vehicle 251 onwards, the assembly plants outfitted new Panthers with the 700bhp Maybach HL230 P30 engine instead of the original HL210. While this added power did not increase the overall speed of the Model D Panther, it did improve acceleration and cross-country performance; above all, it eased the excessive strain frequently imposed on HL210-equipped tanks and thus went some way to improving the mechanical reliability of the tank.

Despite the extensive DEMAG rebuild programme, further field trials undertaken during May with the first 250 Panthers continued to reveal serious problems. Consequently, from June new HL230-engined tanks underwent further modification, while existing vehicles were modified at Grafenwöhr. One of these alterations involved strengthening the tank's over-strained road wheels by fitting additional rivets between the existing 16 rim bolts. In addition, these vehicles underwent further alterations to their transmissions. Meanwhile, back at the factories, some of the new HL230-engined tanks completed during this month emerged without the characteristic set of three smoke-grenade launchers on each side of the turret, although Henschel-manufactured tanks still had them into June. The factories discontinued this feature because field trials had shown that surprise attacks by enemy small-arms fire often inadvertently triggered the smoke grenades when the vehicle still had its hatches open, and the smoke soon incapacitated the crew. By 31 May, the Army had received 250 HL210-engined and 118 HL230-engined Model D tanks. However, many Panthers remained non-operational either because of the faults identified above or because they were being rebuilt and thus could not be deployed at the front for the imminent German summer offensive. Indeed, it was not until further modification work had been completed

in late June, that the Germans managed to redeploy 200 Panthers to the Soviet Union for the now much-delayed German Citadel offensive.

The Panther made its operational debut on 5 July 1943 during Citadel, in which the High Command expected the 200 Panthers to contribute decisively to the stunning victory it expected to secure. Citadel involved a double-pronged German attack from the northern and southern shoulders of a large Soviet salient that jutted west into the German lines around Kursk. The Soviets, however, had detected the German preparations and had built up awesome defensive strength to resist the attack. This build-up did little to perturb German confidence; after all, given the widespread German belief in the combat power of the Panther tank, they simply reckoned that the greater the Soviet force deployed against them, the greater the victory they would achieve once their double pincers had linked up at Kursk to form the largest encirclement yet achieved in the war. The Panther units employed in Citadel – the 51st and 52nd Panzer Battalions – each fielded four companies of 22 Panthers, plus a further eight Model D tanks, to make a total unit strength 96 Panthers each. The two battalions came under the control of General von Lauchert's improvised brigade staff, itself equipped with eight Panthers, which fought alongside the Panzergrenadier Division Grossdeutschland as part of the southern prong of the attack.

Major problems, however, dogged the contribution made by the Panthers even before the offensive began. Because the two Panther-equipped tank battalions were deployed in the East just a few days before Citadel commenced, the units had little time for acclimatisation training in situ. Moreover, 16 tanks broke down on the short journey between disembarking from their transportation trains and reaching the front. Things went little better once the offensive began. In the face of fanatical Soviet resistance, large numbers of Panthers fell by the wayside. By 7 July 1943, the third day of the offensive, just 40 of the 184 Panthers that started Citadel were still operational, while by 10 July just 10 of them

The star antenna mounted on the left rear hull decking, the two-rod antennae, and the drum cupola identifies this vehicle as a Model D Sdkfz 267 Command Panther. Note the Panther's eight pairs of interleaved large road wheels, with four outer and four inner wheels on each side. (The Tank Museum, 510/E5) remained in front-line service. Of the remaining 174 Panthers that had begun Citadel, 23 had been lost due to 'brewing up' after enemy hits on their relatively vulnerable side armour, while two had burned after engine fires before combat had even been joined. Another 44 Panthers were being repaired after mechanical failure and a further 56 because of damage caused by enemy fire or anti-tank mines. German workshops had already repaired a further 40 Panthers with minor damage or mechanical problems, but these were still on the way to rejoin the brigade. The remaining nine tanks, which had been abandoned on the battlefield after sustaining damage, had still to be recovered.

The much vaunted debut of the Panther had proven to be a debacle. Admittedly the Germans could discern a few glimmers of hope from this serious setback. Post-combat reports from the fighting experienced at Kursk confirmed the anticipated combat power of the 7.5cm Panther gun; this weapon had accounted for many T-34 tanks, often at ranges of 1500m or more. In addition, the Panther's two machine guns had proven to be very reliable, with a very low incidence of jamming. However, most of the other aspects of the Panther mentioned in post-combat reports proved unfavourable. Troops observed, for example, that the Panther's turret grenade launchers soon became inoperative due to enemy small-arms fire, that its engine regularly broke down, that its over-stressed transmission often failed, and that its road wheels sometimes fractured. In addition, crews complained about fuel pump leaks that often led to dangerous fires starting inside the tank, the dangerous build-up of gun exhaust gases inside the turret, and the problems caused when driving rain entered the turret through the mantlet binocular periscope. Further modifications were needed, the Germans concluded, before the Panther realised the potential it clearly possessed to be a potent tank on the future battlefield.

Meanwhile back in Germany, even as Citadel unfolded, the factories introduced further production simplifications designed to raise production rates. The new Model D Panthers that rolled off the production

The Germans intended to mount the Narrow Turret (Schmalturm), seen here in England during 1970, in the Panther Model F. Walther Spielberger contends that they also considered mounting the Schmalturm – rather than the Narrow Gun Mantlet Turret suggested by Tom Jentz – in the proposed Panther II. (The Tank Museum, 43/E2)

lines that month no longer had the circular communications hatch fitted to the left-hand side of the turret, and had only one headlamp (on the left) instead of two. From late July, in response to the lessons gathered at Kursk, some newly completed Model D tanks featured more resilient road wheels fitted with 24 rim bolts instead of 16. In addition, these vehicles sported an additional ring mounted on the commander's cupola onto which an anti-aircraft machine gun could be fitted. Yet at this time Panther production still remained hurried and poorly organised; consequently some of the 115 Panthers produced during August did not incorporate these modifications because of over-hasty production or shortages of parts at the factories.

Most of the 115 new Model D Panthers delivered in August – some 96 vehicles – arrived in the East at the end of the month to completely re-equip the 51st Panzer Battalion, which in the aftermath of Citadel had given up its few remaining tanks to reinforce the remnants of the 52nd Battalion. Between them these battalions had suffered 58 Panthers lost by the end of Citadel, excluding another 50 in short-term repair. Yet far worse was to transpire. In the desperate defensive battles the Germans fought to resist the Soviet counter-offensives that erupted over the following six weeks these battalions lost a further 98 Panthers; consequently, fewer than 44 of the original Model D tanks dispatched to Citadel remained operational by early September.

Meanwhile, during September 1943, the lessons learned from the disappointing debut of the Panther at Kursk led to further modifications to the last Model D tanks of the original 850-unit production run. Many of the last 37 Model D Panthers produced in September, for example, featured Zimmerit anti-magnetic mine paste, a substance that hindered Soviet infantry from placing magnetic hollow-charge devices onto the tanks' surfaces. In addition, the late Model D tanks had two new features – a rain guard mounted over the gun sight on the turret mantlet to keep out driving rain, and improved tracks that sported chevron cleats for enhanced traction. As these last Model D tanks emerged, the Panther production firms completed their development work on a successor vehicle, the Model A Panther, which was a slightly modified Model D chassis with an improved turret design. By September the first Model A tanks were going into service alongside the 600 or so remaining Model D tanks.

Although production of the Model D stopped in September 1943 after the 850th vehicle had been completed as per the contract, these tanks continued to serve at the front – alongside their successor Model A and G tanks – right up until the end of the war.

The redesigned hemispherical commander's cupola of the Model A Panther, which contrasted with the drum-shaped version on the Model D tank, included seven periscopes protected by armoured cowlings that improved the field of vision obtained from within the turret. (The Tank Museum, 5/C2)

This mid-production Model A Panther, seen at MAN's Nuremberg factory in January 1944, has 24 rim bolts on its road wheels (rather than the 16 bolts seen on most Model D tanks), and radial-pattern fan louvers on the hull rear decking (instead of the spiral ones mounted on early Model D tanks). (The Tank Museum, 2388/E6)

Obviously, the number of Model D Panthers in service continually declined as losses ate into the numbers remaining, and so by 1945 only a handful of Model D Panthers remained. During autumn 1943, three new Panther units that fielded significant numbers of Model D tanks served in the East, including the II Battalion, SS Panzer Regiment 2 of the Das Reich Division. During September 1943, SS-NCO Ernst Barkmann joined the 4th Company, II Battalion, SS Panzer Regiment 2. This division had recently been re-equipped with Panther Model D tanks, and in bitter defensive battles fought around the Ukraine that autumn, Barkmann's Model D tank performed sterling service before eventually being knocked out. Subsequently, in early 1944, the SS Das Reich Division redeployed to Bordeaux in southern France for refitting with new Model A and G Panthers after incurring heavy losses during recent bitter battles in the East. During this process, Barkmann – now commander of the 4th Company – received a new Model A command tank, vehicle number 424.

The discussion so far has centred on standard Model D combat tanks, but it should be noted that throughout the nine months of the Model D Panther production run, German firms made about ten per cent of them into command tanks, or Befehls Panthers. These vehicles mainly served as commander's and adjutant's vehicles at company, battalion and even regimental levels. The Command Panther was simply a slightly modified standard Panther with ammunition stowage reduced from 79 to 64 rounds to make space for the powerful communications equipment and associated systems they carried. MAN alone completed 63 of these vehicles between January and August 1943. Model D, A and G Command Panthers came in two similar but distinct forms, although both versions shared many common features, such as an additional generator set, the absence of the co-axial turret machine gun, and the addition of three tubes fitted onto the hull sides in which spare antennae rods were housed.

The standard Sdkfz 267 Command Panther, irrespective of whether it was a Model D, A or G, featured the standard battle tank communications device, the Fu 5 10-watt transmitter and ultra-short wavelength receiver. Unlike on the combat tank, however, this device here worked through a two-metre-long rod antenna usually mounted on the right turret rear, adjacent to the commander's cupola, in addition to the standard rod antennae mounted on the left hull decking behind the turret. In normal tactical conditions, operators could expect to obtain a range of eight kilometres with this device. In addition, the Sdkfz 267 tank also mounted the powerful Fu 8 long-range device. This 30-watt transmitter and medium wavelength receiver operated on the frequency band 0.83–3.0MHz, and worked through a distinctive 1.4 metre star antenna normally mounted on the hull roof at the rear of the vehicle. The Fu 8 could communicate up to a maximum range of 65km, sufficient to secure effective communications with regimental and divisional staffs in almost every conceivable tactical situation.

In total, throughout the war, the Germans delivered 350 Sdkfz 267 Command Panthers, including roughly 75 Model D and 200 Model A versions. In addition, it should be remembered that front-line troops could convert standard Panthers to command versions in the field with a dedicated conversion kit if their command vehicles had been destroyed and no replacement was forthcoming. The Sdkfz 267 Command Panther proved highly effective; by retaining the standard Panther gun and armour, it could engage the enemy directly while simultaneously controlling the actions of the unit it commanded. Moreover, by looking like the standard Panther tank its battlefield

French forces pressed into service this captured mid-production Model A Panther, identified by the Kugelblende 50 ball mount in the right hull glacis plate, but only after fitting a new machine gun into the mount – the Panther's MG 34 did not project so far beyond the glacis. (The Tank Museum, 2390/D1)

On this early Model A Panther can be seen the initial layout of the vehicle's rear, with two exhaust pipes and the lack of a jack mounted between them. Note also the two large stowage bins fitted at the sides of the rear plate, a feature common to all Panthers. (The Tank Museum, 2388/F1)

survivability improved, as striving to knock out enemy command tanks had always been a preferred tactic of armoured warfare.

The much less common Sdkfz 268 'Flivo' Befehls Panther command variant was a dedicated air–ground liaison vehicle used for arranging tactical air support for Panther units. Rather than using the Fu 8, this vehicle mounted the Fu 7 device in addition to the standard Fu 5. The Fu 7 was a 20-watt transmitter and ultra-short wavelength receiver that operated on the frequency band 42.1–47.8MHz through a 1.4 metre rod antenna normally mounted on the rear hull roof. In theory, the two (or possibly three) rod antennae of the Sdkfz 268 easily distinguished this vehicle from standard Panther combat tanks (with only one rod antenna) and the Sdkfz 267 Command Panther with one star and either one or two rod antennae. However, pictorial evidence reveals that the Sdkfz 267 and 268 command vehicles often featured non-standard positioning of their aerials, making definite identification problematic. The 'Flivo' Command Panther remained a very rare vehicle, with only 40 being completed by the end of the war. Indeed, given the increasingly adverse strategic situation under which the Luftwaffe laboured during 1944–45, it remains unclear whether many such vehicles actually fulfilled their intended air–ground liaison role, as German tactical air support by this time was extremely limited at best. Moreover, as both the Command Panther variants carried two mounting devices onto which the Fu 7 or Fu 8 could each be fitted, it seems highly likely that the Germans refitted some Sdkfz 268 'Flivo' vehicles as much needed standard command tanks by simply replacing the Fu 7 device with the Fu 8 set.

PANTHER II

During summer 1942, even as MAN began manufacturing its two Versuchs Panther pre-production tanks, the High Command had already grown concerned that the level of protection the new tank possessed might prove insufficient for the combat conditions likely to emerge on the Eastern Front in the immediate future. The initial German response was to investigate the feasibility of adding 20mm-thick bolt-on armoured plates to strengthen the vehicle's protection, as had been done previously with the Panzer III and IV tanks. However,

MAN soon discovered that such work presented extraordinary technical problems that effectively precluded up-armouring the existing Model D design in this manner.

This setback forced the Germans in December 1942 to begin thinking of a new Panther version – the 47-tonne Panther II – that had thicker homogenous armoured plates. The Panther II was to have 100–150mm-thick turret and hull frontal armour instead of the 80–100mm thickness on the Model D. In addition, its side armour was to have 60mm-thick plates instead of the 40mm plates carried by the Model D. Controversy still exists today as to the precise details of the Panther II project, in part because there remains ambiguity in the extant German documentation. Tom Jentz has argued that in December 1942 the Panther II design remained identical to that of the Model D except for the thickness of the armour. Walther Spielberger, in contrast, believes that from its very inception the Germans intended the Panther II to incorporate significant features that would distinguish it markedly from the Model D.

Jentz argues that it was only during mid-February 1943 that the Germans altered the initial Panther II design to make it more than just an up-armoured Model D. For now, the High Command decided that the new tank would incorporate many features of the Panzer-kampfwagen VI Model B King Tiger heavy tank then being designed by Henschel, as well as have a completely new turret design. Spielberger, however, believes that commonality with the King Tiger was a key inspiration behind the Panther II design from its first inception in late 1942. Irrespective of these debates, both scholars agree that by spring 1943 the Panther II design incorporated features of the King Tiger, including the 700bhp Maybach HL230 engine, and resilient steel-tyred, rubber-cushioned, large road wheels. While the King Tiger would mount nine pairs of these road wheels, the Panther II would have seven pairs of identical wheels. The original Panther, in contrast, had eight pairs of non-steel-tyred road wheels. Even the 60cm-thick tracks of the Panther II would act as the narrow (trans-portation) tracks for the King Tiger. Incorporation of these features raised the weight of the Panther II to 51 tonnes. During February 1943, the High Command contracted DEMAG to commence development work on the Panther II, then slated to enter service

This mid-production Model A Panther shows the two cooling pipes fitted to the left exhaust pipe in vehicles completed after early January 1944, as well as the jack mounted between the exhaust pipes. (The Tank Museum, 2902/E5)

Mid-production Model A Panthers being transported by rail to the East in early 1944. The crew of the lead tank have fitted spare track sections to the vehicle's rear hull sides, although increasingly crews mounted these sections on the tank's turret sides to further protect this crucial part of the vehicle. (The Tank Museum, 4704/C4)

in September 1943, and simultaneously informed the existing Panther manufacturing firms that they would continue producing standard Panther tanks only until late 1944, and then switch over to construction of the Panther II.

The health of the Panther II project, however, declined significantly during summer 1943, and in June plans to develop the tank were temporarily halted in favour of continuation of the Model D and Model A production runs. One explanation for this was that the Germans had discovered that by adding Schürzen side skirts to the Model D, the risk posed to the vehicle's 40mm hull side armour was significantly reduced; this development undermined a major justification for developing the Panther II. Consequently, during July 1943, the High Command contracted MAN to produce just two prototype Panther II vehicles. With the impetus for the Panther II project dwindling, and given the many other pressing production demands MAN then faced, development work on the two prototype Panther II tanks languished. Indeed, by the end of the war, MAN had only completed one Versuchs Panther II chassis, but without a turret. The American Army captured this vehicle in the last weeks of the war, fitted it with a recently completed Panther Model G turret, and shipped it off to America, where it remains today on public display.

The turret the Germans earmarked for the Panther II never got beyond the design stage, and today controversy still exists over the precise form it would have taken. Initially the Germans planned to mount in the Panther II the same 7.5cm KwK 42 L/70 gun mounted on the standard Panther tank. Spielberger argues that the Germans intended to mount this gun in the Narrow Turret (Schmalturm) then being developed for the new Model F Panther tank. Jentz, however, argues that the Germans intended to mount a slightly different turret in the Panther II – the Narrow Gun Mantlet Turret. Whatever their precise designs, both turrets sought to reduce the size of the turret front and mantlet, to help increase vehicle survivability. To further complicate the matter, during February 1945 the Germans began work to re-arm a modified version of the Narrow Turret with the 8.8cm KwK 43 L/71 gun of the King Tiger. From this Spielberger contends that if the Germans intended to mount the Narrow Turret in the Panther II, it follows that from spring 1945 they planned that the Panther II would mount the 8.8cm-gunned Narrow Turret and not its original 7.5cm-gunned version. Other plans that the Germans developed later in 1945, however, suggest that they simply intended to mount the 8.8cm-equipped Narrow Turret on any available Model G Panther chassis, to form (in effect) an up-gunned version of the Model F Panther. Clearly, in the chaos that increasingly engulfed the Reich in the last months of the war, the Germans unveiled all sorts of often contradictory plans concerning future tank development. Given that German firms never completed a single Panther II tank, it seems unlikely that these controversies over what turret and main gun the vehicle would have mounted will ever be definitely solved.

PANTHER MODEL A

The second basic Panther design – the Model A – simply comprised the Model D chassis fitted with a redesigned turret. As far back as 18 February 1943 the High Command had decided that once the initial contract of 850 Model D tanks had been completed, subsequent Panthers would have an improved turret design. Although externally the Panther Model D and A turrets looked similar, several features distinguished them: most notably the latter featured a new, up-

Aerial bombing knocked out this Model A Panther at Canisy, near St Lô, in late July 1944, during the American Cobra offensive. Panthers of the SS Das Reich Division, including that led by Barkmann, attempted in vain to halt this successful offensive. (The Tank Museum, 561/A2)

armoured, hemispherical cast commander's cupola as opposed to the drum-shaped cupola of the Model D. The redesigned cupola had seven periscopes protected by armoured cowlings that improved the commander's field of vision, as well as an integral ring for affixing an anti-aircraft machine gun. Another externally visible difference between the two turrets was that on the Model A turret a squared-off joint fitted the turret front plate to the side plates, whereas on the Model D this joint was dove-tailed. In addition to external differences, the Model A turret had a redesigned interior that featured a new variable-speed hydraulic turret traversing system instead of the single-speed one fitted in the Model D. This mechanism produced a turret rotation time of between 15 and 93 seconds, depending on the speed of the engine and the traverse speed ratio selected. In addition, the redesigned turret also had a new bore evacuator that cleared powder gases out of the gun more efficiently than its predecessor.

MNH delivered the first three Model A Panthers in August 1943, and during the following month Daimler-Benz and MAN commenced manufacture of this design after terminating Model D production at the 850th vehicle. Then in September, DEMAG replaced Henschel as the fourth firm involved in Panther production. Between them, these firms produced 149 Model A tanks during September 1943, and subsequently, during the period from December 1943 to March 1944, their deliveries averaged 270 tanks per month. In total, these four firms produced 2200 Model A tanks in a year-long production run that ended in July 1944, when the last 11 Model A vehicles were completed. MNH produced the most vehicles, 830, with Daimler-Benz and MAN constructing 675 and 645 vehicles respectively; DEMAG, however, delivered just 50 Model A Panthers. The factories delivered about 200 of the tanks as Model A Command Panthers with the same communication devices as fitted on the Model D Command variants. Finally, during October 1943–February 1944, the Germans dispatched 300 new Model A tanks to the Königsborn factory for engine rebuilds after reports continued to arrive from the

The distinctive 'wedge' found on the bottom of the hull sides at the vehicle's rear was a characteristic of both Model D and Model A Panthers. However, the Model G variant deleted this wedge in favour of a straight but tapering hull side bottom edge. (The Tank Museum, 2390/B3)

frontline indicating a high incidence of mechanical failures. The modification work necessitated by these continuing problems meant that during winter 1943–44 the Army's receipt of combat-ready Model A tanks fell behind schedule, even though the number of vehicles rolling off the assembly lines was on target.

As with its predecessor, the Model A tank underwent a series of modifications during its year-long production run, the main ones of which are discussed in chronological sequence below. Many of these modifications were intended to simplify and therefore speed up the production process, while others represented responses to post-combat reports received from front-line units. First, from September 1943 onwards new Model A tanks increasingly emerged from the factories with their road wheels strengthened with 24 rim bolts instead of the 16-bolt wheels usually seen on the Model D. Simultaneously, factories began to coat newly completed tanks with Zimmerit anti-magnetic mine paste. Workers applied this thick, cement-like paste, which prevented the enemy fixing magnetic charges to the tank, in a rippled fashion that left a distinctive appearance on vehicles. That same month the assembly plants also incorporated modifications to the Maybach HL230 engine after troops continued to report problems with blown head gaskets and faulty bearings. From January 1944, in an effort to address these continuing mechanical problems, new Panthers featured further modified engines that incorporated an eighth crank shaft.

From December 1943, new Model A tanks also began to appear with an externally obvious modification – the machine gun port in the glacis plate was replaced with a Kugelblende 50 ball-mounted weapon that enjoyed a greater field of fire. This mount included a KZF 2 sight for the radio operator, which meant that the operator's periscope sight on the hull roof could be dispensed with. The vehicles also had their binocular TFZ 12 telescopic gun sight in the turret mantlet replaced with the

The 29-degree slope of the hull sides of this mid-production Model G Panther number 308, contrasted with the 40-degree angle of the side plates featured on both previous Panther models. Note the relative thinness of the four outer road wheels, whereas the four inner wheels were roughly twice as thick. (The Tank Museum, 2390/D3) monocular TFZ 12a sight. From that same month, new Panthers also appeared with hull roof armoured plates that had straight sides instead of ones that interlocked with the hull side plates. Not all of the sub-component pre-assembly firms adopted this modification, however, and so the final assembly firms continued to deliver tanks with interlocked plates, alongside ones with straight plates, right up to the end of the war.

During December 1943 some new Panthers appeared with the pistol ports in the turret sides removed because they were to be replaced with a Close Defence Weapon mounted on the right rear of the turret roof. Because of production delays, the Close Defence Weapon – which fired grenades, smoke charges and flares – only appeared on Model A Panthers in March 1944, and so for three months newly produced Panthers lacked any close defence capability. Then from January 1944, new Model A Panthers appeared with two cooling pipes added to the left exhaust pipe to help air flow to cool the engine. During June–July 1944, the last eight weeks of Model A production, new Panthers emerged with three sockets fitted onto the turret roof. These allowed troops to mount a 2-tonne jib boom on the tank so that the engine could be removed or a new one off-loaded from a nearby vehicle into the tank.

The first Model A Panthers arrived on the Eastern Front in September 1943 with the II Battalion, Panzer Regiment 23, when a handful of these new tanks joined a recently rebuilt battalion dominated by Model D vehicles. Then in October, the II Battalion, Panzer Regiment 2 arrived in the East with 71 Panthers – most of them Model A vehicles – as part of the 13th Panzer Division. Because of the strategic danger posed by unfolding Soviet offensives, the Germans were forced to commit the battalion piecemeal as each company arrived to shore up the hard-pressed front-line defences. After several weeks of this bloody introduction to combat, the Model A crews began to file reports on the tank's performance in these series of bitter tactical engagements. The cupola proved an immediate success, with its enhanced field of vision being welcomed by vehicle commanders. In addition, crews reported

This mid-production Model G Panther reveals two features that distinguished it from its predecessors – the straight but gently sloping bottom edge of the hull sides, and the rotating driver's periscope mounted on the front left hull roof in place of the driver's visor in the left glacis plate. (The Tank Museum, 553/A6)

that the Model A turret was superior to that of its predecessor. On the other hand, front-line units continued to report the high incidence of mechanical failures.

Significant numbers of Model A Panthers, however, only began to reach the German front during winter 1943–44. The Germans dispatched some of the new tanks to front-line units as replacements, while many went straight to the Reich's tank training schools as part of a major re-equipment programme for Germany's Panzer divisions. In turn, each Panzer division's Panzer III-equipped tank battalion returned to Germany where it received new Model A Panthers, undertook crew retraining, and then returned to its parent formation at the front. Officially, these potent Panther-equipped tank battalions fielded 76 Panther tanks – each of its four companies deployed 17 standard tanks, while five standard and three Command Panthers served in the battalion's staff company. During December 1943, the 1st Panzer Division was the first formation to re-equip its Panzer III battalion with Panthers and return to the front. In the following months further armoured divisions rapidly followed suit, most notably the 2nd and 5th SS Panzer Divisions Das Reich and Wiking. Consequently, by 31 January 1944 – at which date total Model A production had reached 1183 vehicles – 888 Model A Panthers had already reached the Eastern Front. Of these approximately 340 represented replacements for existing Panther-equipped units at the front, while the remaining 550 tanks formed six new Panther-equipped battalions that previously had fielded the now obsolete Panzer III tank.

Model A and G Panthers featured identical commander's cupolas, but the fan louver pattern on this tank and its lack of a conical fitting on the turret roof in front of the cupola just below the prominent spike of the sighting vane identifies it as a late Model G tank. (The Tank Museum, 2903/B2)

By February 1944, therefore, most Panther-equipped battalions at the front overwhelmingly fielded Model A tanks, although a few old Model D variants continued to see service throughout 1944. After March 1944, however, Germany's Panther battalions began to receive deliveries of the new Model G variant; subsequently, as attrition gradually denuded the number of Model A tanks still available during 1944–45, the Model G became by far the most numerous Panther fielded by front-line German units. Despite the arrival of the improved Model G, however, significant numbers of Model A Panthers continued to provide sterling service throughout the rest of the war. This fact is attested to, for example, by the famous case of SS-NCO Ernst Barkmann.

During September 1943, Barkmann joined the 4th Company, II Battalion, SS Panzer Regiment 2, which had recently been re-equipped with Panther Model D tanks. In early 1944, Barkmann's parent formation –

A: Three-view of early Model D Panther, Germany, February 1943

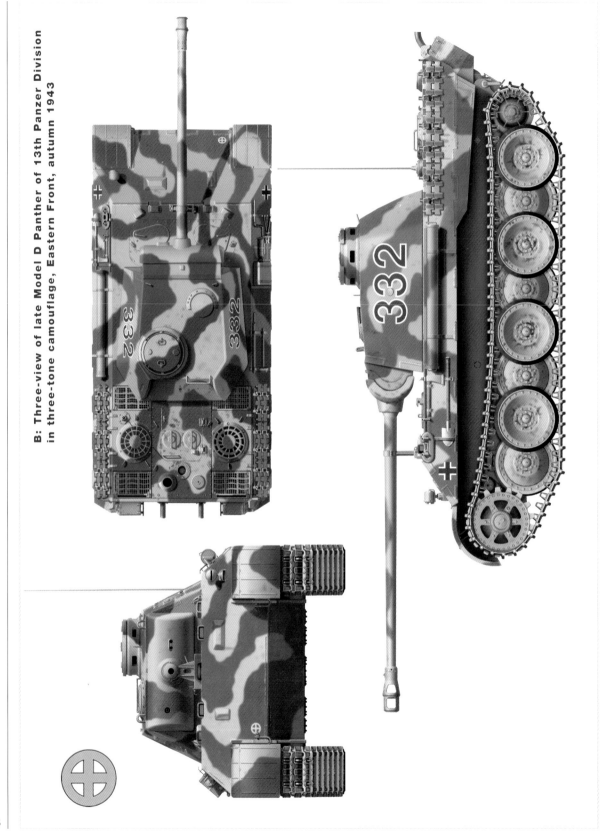

B: Three-view of late Model D Panther of 13th Panzer Division in three-tone camouflage, Eastern Front, autumn 1943

C: Two-view of white-washed early Model A Panther, Eastern Front, winter 1943–44

D: THREE-QUARTER VIEW CUTAWAY OF AN EARLY MODEL G PANTHER IN THREE-TONE CAMOUFLAGE, EARLY SUMMER 1944

KEY

1. Tow cable shackles
2. Steering brakes
3. Mudguard
4. Brake link
5. Sloping hull glacis armour plate
6. Barrel of 7.92mm MG 34 hull machine gun
7. Housing for Kugelblende 50 machine gun ball-mount
8. Stock and trigger for MG 34 hull machine gun
9. Radio operator's armoured periscope
10. Radio operator's hatch
11. Gun barrel travel lock
12. Co-axial 7.92mm MG 34 machine gun (obscured by base of gun barrel)
13. Turret roof
14. Gun mantlet
15. Semi-circular rain guard protecting gun-sight mantlet aperture
16. Main armament compensator
17. Gun cradle
18. TFZ 12a monocular telescopic gun sight
19. Sighting vane
20. Mounting ring for anti-aircraft machine gun
21. Armoured periscope on commander's cupola
22. Hatch in commander's cupola
23. Rod antenna
24. Commander's cupola
25. Turret traversing gear
26. Elevator hand-wheel
27. Commander's headset
28. Armour-piercing ammunition for 7.5cm gun
29. Cylindrical external casing for main armament cleaning kit
30. Engine ventilation grills
31. Spare track sections
32. Sloping lower rear hull sides (trademark of Model G Panther)
33. Road wheel rim-bolts
34. Maybach engine
35. Gunner's seat
36. Interleaved road wheels
37. Co-axial machine gun firing pedal

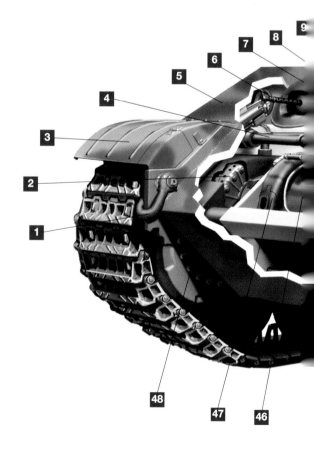

38. Compressor
39. Hydraulic traversing unit
40. Front sprocket wheel
41. Track
42. Headlight
43. Driver's instrument panel
44. Final drive
45. Radio racks
46. AK 2-700 gearbox
47. Track brake cooling duct
48. Lower hull front armour plate
49. 7.5cm KwK 42 L/70 main armament
50. Double baffle muzzle brake

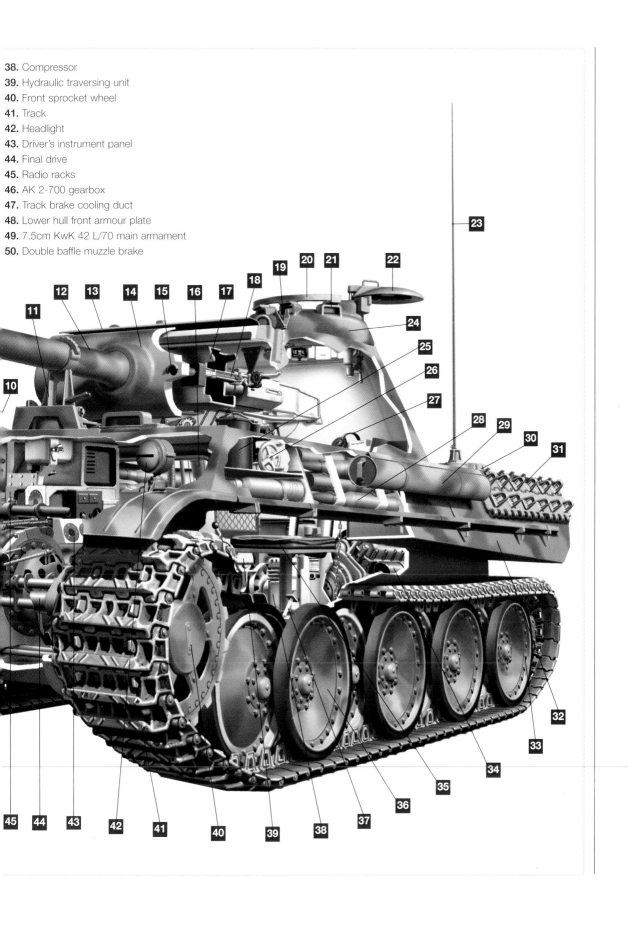

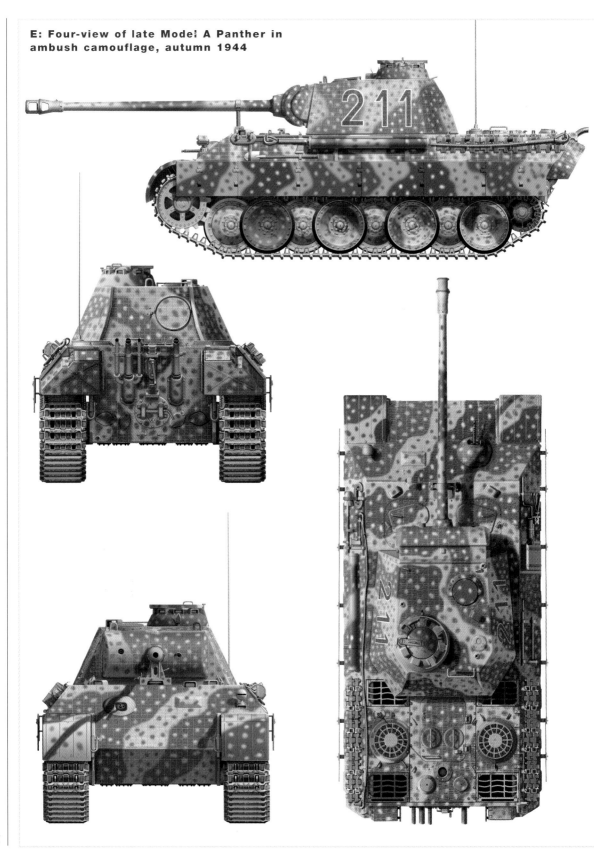

E: Four-view of late Model A Panther in ambush camouflage, autumn 1944

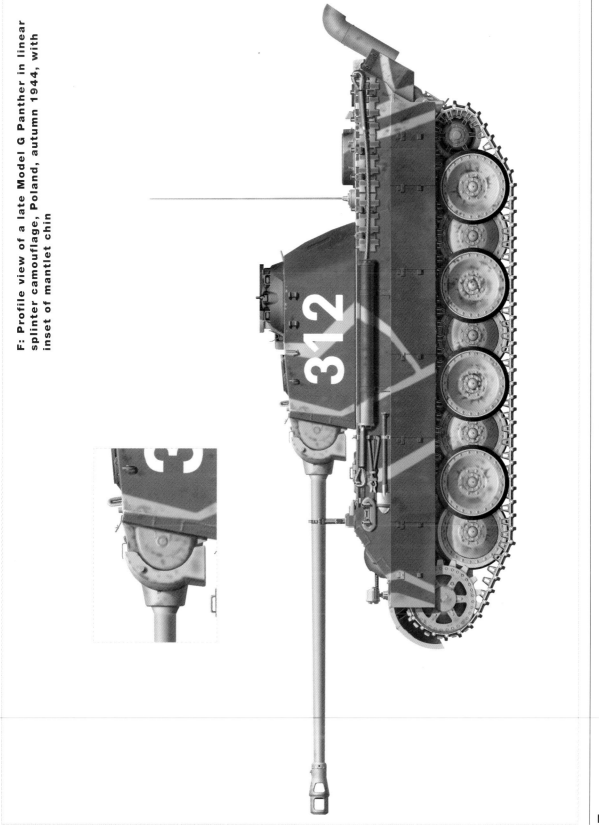

F: Profile view of a late Model G Panther in linear splinter camouflage, Poland, autumn 1944, with inset of mantlet chin

F

G: Three-quarter view of artist's impression of
Model F Panther, Germany, mid-May 1945

the SS Das Reich Division – was re-deployed to southern France for refitting with new Model A and G Panthers after incurring heavy losses in the East. In the days following the 6 June Allied landings in Normandy, the division moved north and joined the German defensive line in the vicinity of St Lô. On 8 July 1944, Barkmann's 4th Company spearheaded a German counter-attack, during which his Model A command tank – vehicle 424 – knocked out its first American Sherman tank. In the bitter defensive battles that raged during 9–12 July, Barkmann's potent 7.5cm cannon destroyed a further five Sherman tanks before a hit by an Allied anti-tank gun forced his tank into the divisional workshops for repairs.

This late Model G Panther sports a redesigned rear hull decking layout and large sheet-metal guards fitted around each exhaust pipe. German factories incorporated the latter modification after early June 1944 to help conceal the tell-tale glow given off by hot exhausts at night. (The Tank Museum, 2390/C6)

On 27 July 1944, Barkmann's tank found itself cut off from the rest of the division by the rapid advances achieved by the American Cobra offensive. During that day, Barkmann's by now damaged Panther nonetheless managed to knock out nine Shermans in a famous break-out attempt now known as the battle of Barkmann's Corner, and the next day he successfully rejoined his parent formation near Coutances. In the bitter defensive stands that raged over the next two days Barkmann accounted for another 15 Allied tanks before having to abandon his burning tank on 30 July. His crew nevertheless managed to escape on foot to fight another day. Re-equipped with a new Model G tank, Barkmann would go on to add further 'kills' to his personal tally during the mid-December 1944 German Ardennes counter-offensive. Although destruction or abandonment was the fate of most remaining Model A tanks during winter 1944–45, it remains clear that small numbers of Model A Panthers that somehow had managed to survive over a year of front-line service continued to offer fierce resistance to the Allied advance right up to the very last days of the war.

PANTHER MODEL G

During May 1943, the Germans decided to postpone the intended start date for Panther II production and hence continue manufacturing the standard Panther design. Consequently, the High Command asked MAN to develop a new Panther variant – the Model G – that incorporated some of the features intended for the future Panther II. The Model G Panther, therefore, mounted the Model A turret on a modified chassis that lacked the downward wedge of the hull sides at the vehicle's rear. In profile, therefore, this new entzwickelte ('straightened') chassis featured a straight hull side bottom edge that tapered gently downwards towards the rear of the vehicle.

In addition to this obvious modification, the Model G incorporated internal changes that resulted in its hull side plates being sloped at 29 instead of 40 degrees. To maintain the level of protection possessed by the Model A tank, the designers increased the thickness of these plates from 40mm to 50mm, which added 0.3 tonnes to the vehicle. The designers, however, did not want the Model G to be heavier than the 44.8-tonne Model A, and so to compensate they decreased the thickness of the lower hull front plates to 50mm, and that of the forward belly armour to 25mm. The increased space created by these modifications allowed the Model G to carry 82 main armament rounds instead of the 79 rounds carried in previous Panthers. Other visible changes incorporated into the Model G included the removal of the driver's visor in the glacis plate in favour of a rotating periscope, and a redesign of the driver's and radio operator's hatches on the front hull decking. Alterations to the rear of the vehicle included a new layout for the rear hull deck and modified twin exhaust pipes. Despite these modifications, however, the general performance of the Model G remained almost identical to that of its predecessor.

In early 1944, while Daimler-Benz and MNH continued producing the Model A, MAN switched to produce the new Model G version, the first examples of which appeared in March. During the next month MAN delivered 105 Model G tanks, while in May Daimler-Benz delivered its first examples of this new variant, having halted production of the Model A. Then in July 1944, MNH delivered its first Model G tanks, by which time production of the Model A had completely ended. German firms constructed a total of 2943 Model G Panthers during a run that lasted 14 months from March 1944 to April 1944, with MAN producing 1143 tanks, Daimler-Benz 1004, and MNH 806 vehicles.

Model G production peaked in July 1944 at 368 vehicles, but thereafter the impact of Allied strategic bombing held monthly delivery rates down to 275–350 for the rest of 1944. The Daimler-Benz factory in Berlin-Marienfelde suffered heavy damage from Allied bombing during 23–24 August, and that at MAN during October–November. During 1945, as part of a wider collapse of the German war economy, Model G deliveries fell sharply to just 128 tanks completed during February, 66 in March, and 49 during April, after which the advancing Allies overran the Panther factories. In

This late Model G Panther, constructed by British forces in mid-1945, is today displayed at the Tank Museum, Bovington. Two of the three small jib boom sockets fitted on Panthers from June 1944 can be seen on the rear right and central left of the turret, as can a conical fitting in front of the cupola underneath the sighting vane. The purpose of the latter device remains unclear, but it may have been connected with the unrealised German intention to mount infra-red equipment on the cupola. (The Tank Museum, 2391/C2)

October 1944, after the factories had delivered 1620 Model G tanks, the Germans announced plans to produce a further 2650 (to make a total of 4270 vehicles) before its successor – the Model F Panther – entered service after May 1945. Sustained Allied aerial attacks, however, held down Model G production to about 1300 vehicles – less than half the earmarked total – and prevented a completed Model F tank from ever reaching the battlefield.

In late April 1945, the German Army received the last Panther tank ever delivered, when the Daimler-Benz factory in Berlin rushed a completed Model G to the troops defending the capital. According to Jentz, the Germans delivered a total of 5943 Panther tanks – including 350 command variants – during a 28-month production run from January 1943 to April 1945. This total comprised 850 Model D Panthers, 2200 Model A vehicles, and 2943 Model G tanks. Spielberger's study, on the other hand, states that the Germans completed 6042 Panthers, of which MAN completed 2042, Daimler-Benz 1982, MNH 1838, Henschel 130 and DEMAG just 50.

As with previous Panther models, the Germans regularly introduced modifications to the Model G during its production run. From May 1944 onwards, new tanks featured welded guards to protect the base of the exhaust pipes at the hull rear. Next, from June, new Panthers were fitted with circular sheet-metal covers around the exhaust pipes to conceal the glow given off at night by hot exhausts. That same month, new examples of this variant also appeared with three sockets welded to the turret roof, to which troops could fit a jib boom so that the vehicle's engine could be removed for repairs. Subsequently, from August 1944, newly completed Panthers had a rain guard mounted over the driver's periscope, as driving rain entering the turret had caused problems for the crew. During that summer, German post-combat reports had also suggested that when the Panther's turret was in certain positions, the driver's and radio operator's hatches could become obstructed, thus preventing the rapid escape of the crew in an emergency. From August, therefore,

Model G tanks had redesigned driver's and radio operator's hatches; during an emergency the crew could simply detach both hatches and slide them aside to escape. Commencing that same month, many new Model G tanks also featured a sheet-metal guard welded to the front of the turret roof to prevent debris becoming lodged in the gap between the top of the mantlet and the turret front.

During September 1944, the factories ceased coating completed Model G vehicles with Zimmerit anti-magnetic mine paste, because of rumours that, when hit, the coating

This close-up view of the rear left side of a Panther turret underneath the commander's cupola reveals the uneven texture left by Zimmerit paste. The vehicle has been captured by British forces, who are here inspecting their prize. (The Tank Museum, 2903/C1)

caused vehicle fires. Next, from October the manufacturers began to deliver finished Panthers in their original red oxide primer, with just a few patches of Olive Green, Red-Brown and Dark Yellow camouflage added. That same month, the Germans added an elongated rain guard for the gun sight visor on the mantlet, as driving rain was still found to cause problems when entering the sight. That autumn, the assembly factories also outfitted small numbers of Model G Panthers with infra-red night fighting equipment, as previously described in Osprey New Vanguard 22, *Panther Variants 1942–45*. Next, from September 1944 onwards, the factories fitted some Panthers with a 'chin' along the bottom of the gun mantlet that prevented incoming rounds being deflected down into the hull roof. During this period, a few Panthers also appeared that featured the more resilient steel-tyred road wheels used in the King Tiger and earmarked for the Panther II. Moreover, during the last weeks of the war, MAN produced a few Model G tanks that had a solitary pair of steel-tyred road wheels at the rear station alongside seven pairs of ordinary rubber-tyred wheels, either to compensate for particularly heavy wear on this station, or simply because there was a shortage of available rubber-tyred wheels. Finally, the last modification incorporated into the Model G before production ended in April 1945 was a new exhaust muffler that reduced the problem of the glow sometimes generated by tank exhausts at night.

During winter 1944–45, the Model G Panther became a key asset with which the increasingly hard-pressed German Army fought its last series of defensive battles. As with all the Panther models, German tank units of this period fielded Model D, A, and G Panthers without distinction. However, after summer 1944, Model G tanks dominated Panther-equipped units as high attrition rates made Model D vehicles exceedingly rare and Model A tanks increasingly uncommon. In such

defensive actions, the potent 7.5cm gun of the Model G provided sterling service. The desperate rearguards enacted by the Panther battalion of the 5th SS Panzer Division Wiking, for example, helped slow down the headlong advance of the Soviet Bagration offensive in White Russia during July–August 1944. During this same period, on the Western Front, the fanatical defensive stands enacted by the 57 Model G Panthers fielded by the teenage Nazis of the 12th SS Panzer Division Hitler Youth did much to slow down the Western Allied advance from the D-Day bridgeheads deep into Normandy. Indeed, right until the very last weeks of the war, whether it was the defence of the surrounded Ruhr industrial zone or of the Seelöwe Heights in front of Berlin, Model G Panthers continued to dominate the determined rearguard stands made by an Army now in its last moments of survival.

But the Army's employment of the Model G was not restricted to defensive actions; indeed, a key battle in which Panthers played a crucial role was rather a surprise counter-offensive – the Battle of the Bulge, the German mid-December 1944 Ardennes campaign. This operation aptly demonstrates the strengths and weaknesses of the Model G Panther. Back in September 1944, after the advancing Western Allies had stalled short of Germany's borders, Hitler decided to launch a surprise counter-attack in the Ardennes that would seize the vital port of Antwerp. On 16 December, 399 Panthers and 551 other AFVs of Army Group B initiated this counter-blow, spearheaded in the north by SS Colonel-General 'Sepp' Dietrich's 6th Panzer Army. The Germans chose to attack in the hilly, wooded Ardennes because its unsuitability for armoured operations meant that the Americans had defended this sector only weakly. Though Hitler insisted that his forces advance 153km to seize Antwerp and thus cut off Montgomery's forces from the Americans to his south, his spearhead commanders recognised that their forces remained too weak – especially logistically – to secure this ambitious objective.

On 16 December 1944, Dietrich's forces broke through the American defences and thrust west toward the River Meuse bridges south of Liége, spearheaded by SS Lieutenant-Colonel Joachim Peiper's battle group, part of the SS Leibstandarte Division. SS Major Werner von Pötschke's tank battalion – which included two companies each of 17 Model G Panthers, plus two Sdkfz 267 Command Panthers in the headquarters group – headed Peiper's force. Through the early hours of 17 December, Peiper's spearhead Panthers moved cautiously along a series of narrow muddy Belgian roads towards Honsfeld. To maintain surprise, the Panthers advanced without lights, being guided along the narrow roads by panzergrenadiers walking alongside them with white cloths tied to their rifles. In this way, Peiper's Panthers caught the American garrison of Honsfeld by surprise and overran them. Despite this success, however, the drawback of relying on the Panther's potent firepower in such terrain became obvious; on many occasions the cumbersome tanks had to manoeuvre back and forth for several minutes so that they could make it round the tight corners of these narrow winding roads.

Model G Panthers from SS Panzer Regiment 5 of the SS Panzer Division 'Wiking' joined combat in August–September 1944 to stem the Soviets' exploitation of their stunningly successful Bagration offensive. The nearest vehicle, II011, served in the II Battalion's headquarters staff platoon. (The Tank Museum, 4704/B5)

Nevertheless, Peiper's Panthers continued to push west along poor roads until at midday they took a short cut past Thirimont to the N23 road along a narrow muddy track. Not surprisingly, the lead Panther soon became bogged down as the muddy track passed over waterlogged ground; Peiper's other tanks had no choice but to reverse carefully up the track and then take the longer route through Baugnez. Despite this delay, Peiper's forces reached Ligneuville early that afternoon where, just as a command Panther passed the Hôtel des Ardennes, a concealed Sherman knocked it out with a hit to its flank that made the vehicle burn fiercely. Nonetheless, Peiper's lead Panthers kept advancing, and during the following morning the potent firepower they delivered helped his panzergrenadiers fight their way across the River Amblève at Stavelot. Having eventually negotiated the sharp bends in the narrow lanes adjacent to Stavelot's market square, Peiper's spearhead Panthers dashed west along better roads toward Trois Ponts; here they intended to secure a bridgehead south of the Amblève and west of the River Salm that would facilitate his planned thrust west. As Peiper's lead Panther emerged from under the railway viaduct north of Trois Ponts, however, a brave American 57mm anti-tank gun team fired from close range and disabled the Panther, blocking the German advance, while American engineers blew the Amblève and the Salm River bridges.

These setbacks forced Peiper – who lacked bridging equipment – to race that afternoon along the poor road north of the Amblève toward Stoumont and thence beyond to the Meuse bridges. Then, during the next morning, he launched his Panthers and panzergrenadiers in a series of frontal attacks against the American positions that blocked the road west. In bitter fighting that lasted all day, his Panthers destroyed

13 American AFVs and overran several enemy positions; in the process however, American tank, anti-tank and bazooka fire knocked out five Model G tanks. Three of these fell in close succession at Stoumont station, their burning hulls forming an effective block to any advance further west by Peiper's forces. Indeed, by dawn on the next day, 20 December, powerful American reinforcements had already virtually surrounded Peiper's isolated battle group.

During 22–23 December, Peiper's encircled force – now virtually out of fuel and ammunition – fell back to make a last stand at La Gleize until a relief column arrived. His tank crews dug in and camouflaged their remaining 21 Panthers to form a defensive hedgehog around the village. All day on 24 December, as massed Allied artillery pounded Peiper's positions and his Panthers used up their ammunition, the Germans waited in vain for the arrival of rescue forces. With no sign of relief, Peiper disobeyed his orders to stand and fight; he disabled his remaining AFVs and during the night of 24–25 December his remaining 800 unwounded soldiers left La Gleize on foot for the German lines. Although Peiper's force, with the help of the potent firepower generated by his Panthers, had got further than any other formation in Dietrich's command, even his battle group had not reached the Meuse River bridges, let alone got across them, to realise Hitler's ambitious expectations.

As a postscript to the role played by Model G tanks in the Ardennes, a unique Panther mission should be mentioned. The Germans attempted to compensate for their lack of combat power by employing surprise and confusion as a force multiplier. On 16 December, Dietrich committed SS Colonel Otto Skorzeny's 150th Panzer Brigade to a covert operation. The brigade fielded 10 modified 'Ersatz' Panthers that had been cleverly disguised to resemble American M-10 tank destroyers. Backed by these vehicles, Skorzeny's commandos – some dressed as American military police – infiltrated the American lines to misdirect

The war ended before the Germans could deploy at the front any completed Model F Panthers, the variant that mounted the Narrow Turret (Schmalturm) on a slightly modified Model G chassis. (The Tank Museum, 2907/F3)

Allied traffic and spread confusion. Although initially the commandos did create disruption, the Panthers were not employed in their intended covert role. Subsequently, the Germans committed Skorzeny's modified Panthers to conventional ground operations during which they all soon succumbed to Allied fire.

PANTHER MODEL F

The Model F was the final combat version of the Panther that the Germans intended to introduce during the war, although in reality German factories did not manage to finish a complete Model F tank before the war ended. This variant married the newly developed Narrow Turret (Schmalturm) with its modified 7.5cm L/70 gun to an altered Model G chassis. The latter featured thicker frontal hull roof armour (25–40mm instead of 16–40mm), improved armour casting on the glacis plate surrounding the Kugelblende 50 machine gun ball mount, and modified guides for the sliding driver's and radio operator's hatches. The Germans decided to develop a new turret to replace that of the Model A and G tanks because combat experience had shown that this design sometimes deflected incoming rounds down onto the thin hull roof armour. In addition, the Germans had concluded that the front of the current Panther turret presented too large a target to the enemy. During winter 1943–44, German firms developed two prototype narrow-fronted and better-armoured Panther turrets – the Narrow Gun Mantlet Turret (which Jentz asserts was to be mounted on the Panther II), and the Rheinmetall Narrow Mantlet Turret. As an outgrowth of these designs, during 1944 Daimler-Benz designed a new Narrow Turret (Schmalturm) that the Germans intended to install on a modified Model G Panther chassis to create the Model F variant. The Narrow Turret mounted a slightly modified gun, the 7.5cm KwK 42/1 L/70, together with a co-axial MG 42 (instead of the MG 34 included on previous Panther designs). The turret had a narrow conical gun mantlet and a narrow turret front, as well as 40–150mm-thick armour instead of the 16–100mm plates on the Model G turret.

German firms produced several Experimental Narrow Panther Turrets (Versuchs-Schmalturm) during mid-1944, and then in August mounted one of them on a standard Model G chassis for test purposes. Next, in late October, the High Command issued a production schedule for the Panther F: Daimler-Benz was to produce the first 50 tanks during February 1945, and by May – when Model G construction was to have ended – Krupp, MAN, MNH and Ni-Werk were to join Model F production. But the combination of Allied air strikes and ground advances, plus the administrative chaos engulfing the tottering Nazi Reich, delayed manufacture of the Model F. Consequently, when the Soviets overran the Daimler-Benz factory at Berlin-Marienfelde in late April 1945, they discovered four well-advanced Model F chassis, plus several completed Narrow Turrets. Indeed, during late April, Daimler-Benz did fit several Model G Panther turrets to completed Model F chassis and delivered these tanks to the troops then desperately defending Berlin. Clearly, while the Germans did not manage to finish a single Model F Panther prior to the end of hostilities on 8 May 1945, they remained literally only a few days away from achieving this goal when the Soviets overran the Marienfelde factory. And so with this event ended the story of Germany's Panther medium tank.

THE PANTHER ASSESSED

A tank's overall effectiveness is determined by the combination of five factors. The first is the vehicle's lethality – the penetrative capabilities of its main armament, its accuracy (determined chiefly by the quality of its optical equipment), and the number of rounds carried. The second factor is the tank's battlefield survivability – the degree of protection afforded by its armour. The third is the vehicle's mobility – its ability to move and manoeuvre at speed across various types of terrain, including the ability to cross bridges without them collapsing under its weight, as well as its ability to obtain a reasonable operational range from the fuel carried. The fourth is the tank's mechanical reliability, particularly that of its engine, transmission and suspension. The last factor is the financial and resource costs involved in producing the tank and then maintaining it in an operational state on the battlefield.

When these criteria are considered, it is clear that the Panther was one of the best tanks of the Second World War. Undoubtedly, its most impressive aspect was its lethality. The 7.5cm KwK 42 L/70 gun was a superb weapon, as attested to by the numerous 'kills' obtained in combat at even long range. The gun

This interior view of a Panther tank turret, as seen from the left, shows the gunner's seat in the centre of the picture, while the TFZ periscope remains just out of shot above the top left of the photograph. (The Tank Museum, 11/B5)

carried three main types of ammunition – the PzGr.39/42 armour piercing ballistic-capped (APBC) round, the rare PzGr.40/42 tungsten AP shell, and the SprGr high explosive round. Firing the PzGr.39/42 and 40/42 rounds at the normal combat range of 1000m, the Panther could penetrate 111mm and 149mm-thick armour sloped at 30 degrees, enough to deal with virtually all enemy tanks. In addition, the Panther's excellent TFZ 12 or 12a telescopic sight permitted accurate targeting even at long range. This enabled the L/70 gun to achieve an impressive 97 per cent probability of hitting a target first time at 1000m with the PzGr.39/42 under normal combat conditions; indeed, even at the long range of 2500m, the Panther still obtained a 29 per cent first-hit probability with this round.

The other chief strength of the Panther was its survivability, which rested mainly on its thick, well-sloped frontal armour. The Soviet T-34/85, for example, could only penetrate the Panther frontally at a range of 500m, whereas the 75mm-gunned Sherman M3A2 could not do so even at point-blank range. However, by 1944–45, new threats had emerged – notably the Soviet Josef Stalin and the American Pershing heavy tanks, plus the 17-pounder anti-tank gun – that proved capable of penetrating the Panther frontally at 1500m. The side and rear armour of the Panther, however, remained much more vulnerable, with most Allied tanks being able to penetrate these plates at ranges of 1500m or more. Significantly, with the exception of the JS and Pershing tanks, throughout its operational career, the Panther always proved capable of knocking out opposing tanks at ranges at which the latter were incapable of penetrating the Panther.

The combination of potent firepower and impressive survivability might have made the Panther the most effective tank of the war. However,

Unfinished Panther tank hulls and Jagdpanther heavy tank destroyers can be seen on this production line at one of the five armament factories located in the Reich that manufactured the Panther tank. (The Tank Museum, 4049/C3)

it was less impressive in terms of mobility, reliability and cost; consequently, some scholars believe that the solid all-round performance of the Soviet T-34/85 tank gave it the edge over the Panther as the most effective tank of the war. For in terms of mobility, the Panther's performance was only reasonable. This 44.8-tonne tank had an unimpressive ground pressure of 0.735kg/cm^2, remained relatively underpowered at 15.6bhp/tonne (with the 700bhp engine), and had an unimpressive cross-country range of only 100km. The problems the bulky Panther experienced in confined terrain were aptly demonstrated, as we have seen, by the difficulties Peiper's tanks experienced in the Ardennes. In addition, the Panther was dogged by mechanical reliability problems throughout its career, even though by the time of the Model G these weaknesses had been ironed out to a significant degree. Last, it should also be remembered that the Panther was a complex and sophisticated vehicle that proved both expensive and time consuming to produce – each tank took 2000 man-hours to complete – as well as to maintain in the field.

The combination of these three factors served to undermine somewhat the superb lethality and impressive survivability delivered by the Panther. Nevertheless, it remains clear that the Panther medium tank was one of the most effective of the entire war, and its employment at the front undoubtedly enabled the German Army to resist overwhelming Allied pressure for significantly longer than would otherwise have been possible. Given this effectiveness, it remains surprising that after the end of the war, no more than two dozen captured Panthers saw service in other armies (such as the Bulgarian and French forces). Consequently, it would be fair to say that the impressive operational history of the Panther tank ended in the ruins of Hitler's supposed 1000-year Nazi Reich in May 1945.

COLOUR PLATE COMMENTARY

A: THREE-VIEW OF EARLY MODEL D PANTHER, GERMANY, FEBRUARY 1943

This plate depicts an early Panther Model D tank from February 1943 at the Grafenwöhr tank training school in Germany. This tank served with the 51st or 52nd Panzer Battalions for crew familiarisation training, and is one of the first 22 Panthers constructed. The vehicle is painted throughout with a base coat of Dark Yellow (RAL 7028) paint and lacks any tactical markings. This tank was one of the first German vehicles of this period to sport such a base colour, as the High Command had only just ordered that Dark Yellow (RAL 7028) replace Dark Panzer Grey (RAL 7021) as the standard base paint for German tanks. Several features evident here identify the tank as a Model D Panther. Note the driver's vision port on the left hull plate and the sloping bottom of the hull sides towards the rear of the vehicle, two features subsequently absent in Model G tanks. Next, note the letterbox mount (here closed) for the machine gun in the right hull glacis plate, and the TFZ 12 binocular sight in the left turret mantlet, both of which identify the vehicle as a Model D or an early Model A tank. Last, the commander's cupola on the left turret roof is drum-shaped, which marks the vehicle as a Model D. Several features, moreover, identify this tank as one of the first Model D Panthers constructed. First, note the absence of a ring fitted for an anti-aircraft machine gun on the top of the commander's cupola, a feature that began to appear in July. Second, note the two headlamps on the vehicle's sloping front hull plate – after summer 1943 the right-hand lamp was discontinued. The tank also mounts grenade launchers on the turret sides, and a circular communications hatch in the left turret side, features that were discontinued in July 1943. Furthermore, the tank lacks Schürzen side skirting, suggesting that it was built before April 1943. Finally, the camouflage scheme and lack of tactical markings specifically identifies the tank as one of the first 22 Panthers built – these uniquely featured a clutch-brake steering gear device – which the Army used for training purposes at Grafenwöhr.

B: THREE-VIEW OF LATE MODEL D PANTHER OF 13TH PANZER DIVISION IN THREE-TONE CAMOUFLAGE, EASTERN FRONT, AUTUMN 1943

In this plate can be seen a late-production Model D Panther from the 3rd Company of I/Panzer Regiment 2 of the 13th Panzer Division deployed somewhere on the Eastern Front during autumn 1943. The tank has most of the new design features introduced during the nine-month-long Model D production run. It sports the standard three-tone camouflage pattern of base Dark Yellow (RAL 7028), over which irregular patches of Red-Brown (RAL 8017) and Dark Olive Green (RAL 6003) have been added. In addition, the tank sports an unusually positioned small German cross in black with white outline located at the sloping front of the left hull side just in front of the location where the crew have stowed essential tools such as a hawser and spade. The vehicle's tactical number, 332, is painted in Red with a fairly substantial outline painted in White. Six features distinguish this vehicle as a late Model D. First, the tank has only one headlamp, on the left. Second, it lacks the circular communications hatch fitted to the left-hand side of turret. Third, its road wheels have 24 rim bolts instead of 16. Fourth, it has an additional ring mounted on the commander's cupola onto which an anti-aircraft machine gun could be fitted. Fifth, the vehicle has a wide rain guard mounted over the TFZ 12 binocular gun sight on the turret mantlet to keep out driving rain. Finally, the tank has improved tracks with chevron cleats for enhanced traction in the muddy conditions prevalent on the Eastern Front during autumn. It is interesting to note first that the tank lacks Schürzen side skirts, and second, given the absence of a rippled finish to the vehicle's exterior, that the tank had not been coated with Zimmerit anti-magnetic mine paste, which during this period was increasingly being applied in the field.

C: TWO-VIEW OF WHITE-WASHED EARLY MODEL A PANTHER, EASTERN FRONT, WINTER 1943–44

This plate depicts an early Model A Panther deployed on the Eastern Front during winter 1943–44. As was the practice

This Soviet photograph of a captured early Model D Panther illustrates well the 51st Panzer Battalion's tiger symbol, the circular shape of the gun mantlet, and the form of the three smoke-grenade launchers mounted on each turret side. (The Tank Museum, 22/E1)

ABOVE **Model A Panther, number 501, engaged in combat in the East during early 1944. As often occurred, the tank has lost some of its Schürzen plates, probably due to damage by enemy fire. (The Tank Museum, 4704/C3)**

RIGHT **This Daimler-Benz late Model D Panther, chassis number 211213, seen at the 15th Panzer Division training area at Sagan during autumn 1943, featured Schürzen skirting plates mounted on the side of the vehicle to protect the track and hull sides from enemy fire. (The Tank Museum, 341/H6)**

during wintry conditions, the crew have white-washed the tank with White Emulsion (TL 6345) to blend in with the snow and ice; however, in this case they have done this quite crudely, thus leaving a rather uneven effect with occasional faint glimpses of the original Dark Yellow (RAL 7028), Red-Brown (RAL 8017) and Dark Olive Green (RAL 6003) three-tone base camouflage just showing through. The crew, again following common procedure, have painted the vehicle's tactical number, 226 (which identifies it as the sixth tank of the second troop of the second company in this unknown unit) in Red with a thin White outline. It is interesting to note that for whatever reason, the crew have made no attempt to white-wash either the spare track or the tools carried on the tank's hull sides. The Model A tank was essentially a Model D chassis mounted with a new turret. The most obvious new feature, in comparison with the Model D, is the new cast commander's cupola on the left rear of the turret. This cupola has an entirely new

hemispherical shape and has seven armoured periscopes to enhance the commander's field of vision. A more subtle distinction between this Model A and its predecessor can be seen where the side turret plate interlocks with the turret front plate just behind the mantlet; on this tank, this joint is square cut, whereas in Model D tanks the joint was dove-tailed. Further subtle differences can also be seen in the shape of the mantlet in this plate's side view. Apart from these features, the Model A is virtually indistinguishable from its predecessor. This early Model A, unlike later tanks of this design, still features pistol ports in the turret sides, and the TFZ 12 binocular gunner's sight.

D: THREE-QUARTER VIEW CUTAWAY OF AN EARLY MODEL G PANTHER IN THREE-TONE CAMOUFLAGE, EARLY SUMMER 1944

This plate shows a cutaway of an early Model G Panther, delivered in April 1944 but seen here in early summer, with large parts of its interior components on view. The tank's exterior features the standard three-tone camouflage scheme that was increasingly superseded from August 1944 by 'ambush' designs. The former pattern consisted of a base colour of Dark Yellow (RAL 7028), over which random patches of Red-Brown (RAL 8017) and Dark Olive Green (RAL 6003) have been added. The precise features of this basic pattern varied significantly from tank to tank depending on unit practice and the tactical conditions present at that moment. The tank's interior was painted, as standard, in Light Cream (RAL 1001) with interior components in various shades of metallic grey or charcoal, with lettering in Red. The gently sloping straight bottom edge of the rear hull sides identifies this tank as a Model G Panther with its 'straightened' chassis, in contrast to the downward wedge of the rear hull sides seen on previous Model D and A tanks. That this is an early, not a late-production, Model G tank can be discerned by the lack of both a shot-deflecting chin under the mantlet and steel-rimmed road wheels.

E: FOUR-VIEW OF LATE MODEL A PANTHER IN AMBUSH CAMOUFLAGE, AUTUMN 1944

Here a late-production Model A Panther that sports all the features introduced during the production run can be seen just a few months after it was delivered. The vehicle sports the new 'ambush' camouflage, as authorised by the High Command on 19 August 1944, that increasingly replaced the standard three-tone pattern seen in Plate B. The 'ambush' camouflage scheme consisted of a base paint of Dark Yellow (RAL 7028), over which extensive patches of Red-Brown (RAL 8017) and Dark Olive Green (RAL 6003) were added. However, in the 'ambush' pattern the crew first added small white, yellow, or pale grey spots to the tank's Red-Brown (RAL 8017) and Dark Olive Green (RAL 6003) patches and then small green spots to the areas of base Dark Yellow (RAL 7028) that still showed. At least six external modifications evident in this plate differentiate this tank from early Model A vehicles. First, the tank features a Kugelblende 50 ball-mount for its hull glacis plate machine gun instead of the previous letterbox mount. Second, it mounts a TFZ 12a monocular

gun sight in the mantlet (instead of the TFZ 12 binocular version), plus a rain guard to protect the sight from driving rain. Third, the pistol ports in the turret side have been removed. Fourth, twin cooling pipes can be seen to the left exhaust pipe at the vehicle's rear. Fifth, note the three small circular sockets fitted on the turret roof to which the jib boom could be attached. Finally, there is a large circular fitting on the right rear of this tank's turret roof where the Close Defence Weapon was to have been fitted.

F: PROFILE VIEW OF A LATE MODEL G PANTHER IN LINEAR SPLINTER CAMOUFLAGE, POLAND, AUTUMN 1944, WITH INSET OF MANTLET CHIN

A late Model G Panther, dating from after September 1944, can be seen in this plate. This variant's characteristic 'straightened' chassis that lacked the downward wedge of the hull sides at the vehicle's rear, however, cannot be seen here as it is obscured by the Schürzen armoured side skirts. The three features that identify the tank in profile not only as a Model G but as a late-production vehicle, are the distinctive 'chin' fitted to the bottom of the mantlet to prevent incoming rounds being deflected down onto the thin hull roof, together with the modified driver's periscope, and the altered rear hull decking. Unlike some late Model G tanks, however, this vehicle sports the standard rubber-tyred Panther road wheels, not the more resilient steel-rimmed versions. Four other modifications, not evident here, also identify this Panther as a Model G: a redesigned rear hull deck and modified twin exhaust pipes, less sloping hull side plates, modified driver's and radio operator's hatches, and last, a rotating periscope for the driver instead of the visor in the left hull glacis plate. The crew have painted the vehicle's

This early Model G Panther sports redesigned driver's and radio operator's hatches in the front hull roof, and a modified rear hull roof with altered fan louvers. The shape of the driver's periscope on the front left hull roof distinguishes this vehicle from late Model G tanks that featured a larger periscope. (The Tank Museum, 2902/D2)

tactical identification number, 312, in large monochrome White (RAL 9002) on the tank's turret sides. The tank has been camouflaged in a relatively uncommon 'splinter' design, with large straight-edged blocks of Dark Olive Green (RAL 6003) and Red-Brown (RAL 8017) painted over a base colour of Dark Yellow (RAL 7028), only narrow strips of which remain. The whole design is rather reminiscent of the disruptive 'Dazzle Ships' pattern used commonly in warship camouflage schemes. Note also that the crew have made no attempt to camouflage the gun barrel, mantlet, or road wheels, which remain in base Dark Yellow (RAL 7028).

G: THREE-QUARTER VIEW OF ARTIST'S IMPRESSION OF MODEL F PANTHER, GERMANY, MID-MAY 1945

This plate is an artist's impression of what a completed Model F Panther would have looked like had one been delivered to the Army. However, the Soviets captured the Daimler-Benz factory at Berlin-Marienfelde in late April 1945 before this could be achieved. The Soviets discovered in this factory four well-advanced Model F chassis plus several unmounted completed Narrow Turrets (Schmalturm); the Model F Panther would have been created by simply marrying these Narrow Turrets to the completed chassis. The Narrow Turret of the Model F mounted a slightly modified gun, the 7.5cm KwK 42/1 L/70, with a co-axial MG 42 (rather than MG 34), and featured a narrow conical gun mantlet and turret front, plus thicker armour, so as to increase its battlefield survivability. The chassis remained virtually identical to that of the Model G, except that it had enhanced armour casting on the glacis plate surrounding the machine gun ball mount, modified guides for the sliding driver's and radio operator's hatches, and thickened frontal hull roof plates. In this artist's impression, the tank has been painted in Dark Olive Green (RAL 6003) throughout as its base paint, a procedure authorised by the German High Command in late November 1944.

INDEX